Little RIDDLERS

Berkshire

Edited By Sarah Washer

First published in Great Britain in 2018 by:

Young Writers
Remus House
Coltsfoot Drive
Peterborough
PE2 9BF
Telephone: 01733 890066
Website: www.youngwriters.co.uk

FOREWORD

Dear Reader,

Are you ready to get your thinking caps on to puzzle your way through this wonderful collection?

Young Writers' Little Riddlers competition set out to encourage young writers to create their own riddles. Their answers could be whatever or whoever their imaginations desired; from people to places, animals to objects, food to seasons. Riddles are a great way to further the children's use of poetic expression, including onomatopoeia and similes, as well as encourage them to 'think outside the box' by providing clues without giving the answer away immediately.

All of us here at Young Writers believe in the importance of inspiring young children to produce creative writing, including poetry, and we feel that seeing their own riddles in print will keep that creative spirit burning brightly and proudly.

We hope you enjoy riddling your way through this book as much as we enjoyed reading all the entries.

CONTENTS

Our Lady Of Peace Catholic Infant & Nursery School, Slough

Harrison Durkan (7)	59
Apolonia Łucja Marszałek (6)	60
Jigar Saini (6)	61
David Narh-Dorh (7)	62
Musa Asif (7)	63
Mayuri Nathini Das (7)	64
Hadi Asif (7)	65
Coco Janot (7)	66
Sanjana Podigala (7)	67
Aapti Vij (5)	68
Kamsi C Isi (7)	69
Zuzanna Pajdzik (7)	70
Anish Mandal (6)	71
Makayla Korkor Bah-Nartey (7)	72
Simon Maradze (7)	73
Ugochukwu Uchenna Eze (7)	74
Miguel Christopher Quebral (5)	75
Amelia Page (6)	76
Isabelle Ahanon (5)	77
Lauren Fualefac (6)	78
Tianna-Rose Kalirai (6)	79
Annabel Lomas (7)	80
Timizo Nganga (7)	81
Roxi Hasley (5)	82
Bruno Valek (7)	83
Muhammad Ashraf (6)	84
Gabriel Wojchiech Dubiel (7)	85
Sirien Jabr (7)	86

Parlaunt Park Primary School, Slough

Humna Kashif Siddiquei (7)	87
Simranjit Saggu (6)	88
Sahil Bhatia (6)	89
Klaudia Jonderko (6)	90
Sreya Aji (7)	91
Shanzay Aslam (6)	92
Muhammad Salaar Moosa (6)	93
Shaivi Prasad (7)	94
Padmakali Chaudhuri (6)	95

Rayan El-Taki (7)	96
Navin Singh Dhinsay (6)	97
Samardeep Singh Bhagtana (6)	98
Zara Szarvas-Jones (7)	99
Sophie Brennan (6)	100
Rehan Siddique Shahzad (7)	101
Daisy Kirby (7)	102
Walid Alqaysi (7)	103
Gabriel Justin Toma (7)	104
Riley Tearle-Reardon (7)	105
Gurdeep Singh Virdee (6)	106
Safa Ghauri (7)	107
Solha Stoor (6)	108
Ritwik Mukherjee (6)	109
Amelia Eileen Warren-Searle (6)	110
Keira Grace Chopra (7)	111
Noor Awan (7)	112
Billy Edmonds (7)	113
Umayma Hedayet (6)	114
Briony Mcintyre (7)	115

St Michael's CE Primary School, Sunninghill

Benjy Everett (7)	116
India Star McNair (6)	117
Phoebe Powell (7)	118
Anya Carroll (7)	119
Daisy Dyer (7)	120
Connie Neal (7)	121
Isabella Rose Sousa (6)	122
Alexander Cunnison (6)	123
Molly Isabella Stokes (7)	124
Theo Rose (7)	125
Nancy Neal (5)	126
Megan Lloyd (7)	127
Anish Nehra (7)	128
Jessica Smith (5)	129
Zara McSharry (6)	130
Hannah Michelle Williams (5)	131
Poppy Dyer (6)	132
Ethan Smyth (6)	133
Charlie Kemp (6)	134
Theo Simmonds (5)	135

Louis Fowler (5)	136	Caitlin Bonnett (5)	174
Elizabeth Rowat (6)	137	Isaac Stephens (6)	175
Eliza Read (6)	138	Charlie Cox (6)	176

The King's House School, Windsor

Caleb Erasmus (6)	139
Grace Ravelo (7)	140
Jesse Daniel Rademeyer (6)	141
Evelyn Shaya (6)	142
Daniel Richards (6)	143
Jessica Costa (6)	144
Hugo Holmes-Clough (5)	145
Harriet Holmes-Clough (7)	146
Patricio Taylor (7)	147
Elizabeth Harding (6)	148
Alex Welch-Torino (6)	149

Waverley School, Finchampstead

Stephanie Ann Simon (7)	150
Edward Hinitt (6)	151
Eva Hope (6)	152
Eleanor Woolger (6)	153
Leo Lightstone (5)	154
Antar Pabla (6)	155
Imogen Nicol (6)	156
Niki Pittock (6)	157
Sofia Beet (7)	158
Catherine Agar (5)	159
Esmé Walsh (6)	160
Vasu Gupta (6)	161
Sophia Fadden (6)	162
Alessa (6)	163
Hannah Rowsell (6)	164
Jo Tan (5)	165
Imogen Avery (5)	166
Tommy German (5)	167
Fraser Boulton (5)	168
Pippa Ellen Dickinson (5)	169
Beau Murphy (6)	170
Emily Neale (5)	171
Max Sully (5)	172
Lyra Brooks (5)	173

THE POEMS

Nothing

I am in your nightmares.
I am what there was before the universe.
I was there at the beginning,
And I shall be there at the end.
The poor have it.
The rich need it.
What am I?

Answer: Nothing.

Mohammed Hassaan (7)

Jumpy Lumpy

My name starts with the letter G.
I accidentally went to someone's house,
Who I didn't know.
My hair is golden.
I ate everyone's porridge.
They all tasted yucky,
But then a pig came back.
I saw one, I smelt it,
And it smelt good.
I took a bite and it tasted yummy.
I ate it all.
Who am I?

Answer: Goldilocks.

Mahveen Rafay (5)
Emmer Green Primary School, Reading

Locked In A Tower

I have long hair.
I don't like being locked in towers.
My mum is actually the queen.
I am in love.
My hair is golden.
My hair is so long it can reach to the ground
of the tallest tower.
Who am I?

Answer: Rapunzel.

Grace Nicole Isabel Toomey (6)
Emmer Green Primary School, Reading

Off Roaders .20

I am an SUV.
I am the boss of all the SUVs.
I have an SOS button at the top of the driver's seat.
I am a 4-wheel drive.
I can also be a monster truck.
I have seven seats.
What am I?

Answer: A Land Rover.

Sriram Goteti (6)
Emmer Green Primary School, Reading

I'm Scared

We have a house of straw.
We have a house of sticks.
We have a house of bricks,
And we burnt a wolf.
We're pink.
We have a snout.
We have a curly tail.
Who are we?

Answer: The three little pigs.

Taylor James Smith (5)
Emmer Green Primary School, Reading

Double Trouble

We have spots on our cheeks.
We have tiaras.
We live in a big castle.
We are sisters.
We are not very pretty,
But we think we are.
We are very mean.
Who are we?

Answer: *The ugly stepsisters.*

Shauntai Browne (5)
Emmer Green Primary School, Reading

Green Killer

I have three horns.
I have a frill around my neck.
I live in grass,
And eat grass.
I try to get eaten by a T-rex.
I am extinct.
I have a beak.
What am I?

Answer: A triceratops.

James Robert Ross Stoneham (6)
Emmer Green Primary School, Reading

Animals Enemies

We are a cat and a mouse.
The cat chases the mouse.
We are not friends.
The mouse has a secret hideout with a door.
The mouse always wins the fight.
Who are we?

Answer: Tom and Jerry.

Oliver Provoost (5)
Emmer Green Primary School, Reading

Blue Ball

I am blue.
I have a black dot in the middle of me.
I have energy in me.
I have water in me.
I begin with a W,
And there are others of me.
What am I?

Answer: A water energy ball.

Daniel Drury (5)
Emmer Green Primary School, Reading

Fast Runner

I am yellow.
I have black spots.
I am the fastest runner.
I am the fastest runner to hunt for my prey.
I can kill anything.
I can climb up trees.
What am I?

Answer: A cheetah.

Bethan Francesca Thompson (5)
Emmer Green Primary School, Reading

Yellow Monster

I can use my tail.
I can use thunderbolts.
I can use electric through balls.
I have a spiky tail.
My master is Ash.
I am a Pokémon.
Who am I?

Answer: Pikachu.

Harry Phelps-Jones (5)
Emmer Green Primary School, Reading

Chair Breaker

I like to eat porridge.
I broke the chair.
I slept in the smallest bed.
I forgot my manners.
I am scared of bears.
I have golden hair.
Who am I?

Answer: Goldilocks.

Ronit Singhal (5)
Emmer Green Primary School, Reading

A Furry Friend

I have four legs and a tail.
I have fuzzy fur.
My claws are very sharp.
I have long whiskers.
I love to eat fish.
I love to chase mice.
What am I?

Answer: A cat.

Zara Akhter (5)
Emmer Green Primary School, Reading

Who Am I?

I have golden hair.
I brush my hair.
I don't like to be in towers.
I love the sun.
I love nature.
I have a wicked stepmother.
Who am I?

Answer: Rapunzel.

Greta Nagy (5)
Emmer Green Primary School, Reading

Yellow Monster

I have a spike on my tail.
I have a tail wrap.
I am yellow.
I have spikes on my ears.
I have a thunder shock.
I zap people.
Who am I?

Answer: Pikachu.

Isabella Parlour (5)
Emmer Green Primary School, Reading

What Am I?

I am big.
I am tall.
I like eating children.
I live in a castle.
I have lots of gold.
I grind your bones to make my bread.
What am I?

Answer: A giant.

William Foulkes (6)
Emmer Green Primary School, Reading

Beach Combing

I have patterns.
I am on the beach.
Animals used to live in me.
I come in many sizes.
If you hold me, you can hear the sea.
What am I?

Answer: A seashell.

Lois Hambleton (5)
Emmer Green Primary School, Reading

The Best Writing

I have long hair.
I have yellow hair.
I am beautiful.
I live in a tower.
I like having adventures.
I live in a castle.
Who am I?

Answer: Rapunzel.

Laashja Pirathapan (6)
Emmer Green Primary School, Reading

Animal Eater

I have a big, furry mane.
I am from the African wild.
I hunt for my prey.
I have a fierce roar.
I am the king of the jungle.
What am I?

Answer: A lion.

Jina Shah (5)
Emmer Green Primary School, Reading

King Of The Dinosaurs

I eat meat.
I run fast.
I eat dinosaurs.
I have two small arms.
I have a long tail.
I have lots of big, sharp teeth.
What am I?

Answer: A T-rex.

Kian Waite-O'Leary (5)
Emmer Green Primary School, Reading

Cats

I fight tigers.
I can climb trees.
I have very sharp claws.
My fur is black.
The forest is where I make my home.
What am I?

Answer: A black panther.

Harry Rapley (5)
Emmer Green Primary School, Reading

Electric Creature

I shoot lightning.
I am yellow.
I am strong.
My name starts with P.
My friend is Charmander.
I am a Pokémon.
Who am I?

Answer: Pikachu.

Harry Macbeth (5)
Emmer Green Primary School, Reading

What Am I?

I run fast.
I'm tasty.
I meet a fox.
I got rather wet.
I'm small.
I haven't got a house.
What am I?

Answer: The gingerbread man.

Henry Wirgman (6)
Emmer Green Primary School, Reading

Poké Person

I have glasses.
I'm not an animal.
I am a person.
I am in Pokémon.
I am a trainer.
I look after Pikachu.
Who am I?

Answer: Ash.

Riley Joah Siadatan (5)
Emmer Green Primary School, Reading

My Riddle Book

I swim in cold water.
I have two legs.
I have wings.
I am white and black.
I have a beak.
I walk sideways.
What am I?

Answer: A penguin.

Mya Monovskaya (6)
Emmer Green Primary School, Reading

The Lady And The Beast

I like dancing.
I have a yellow dress.
I love the beast.
I wear a gold crown.
I live in a village.
Who am I?

Answer: A princess called Belle.

Ava Tabitha Lily Graham (5)
Emmer Green Primary School, Reading

I Am The King

I have a big mane.
I have a long tail.
I have a big foot.
I eat meat.
I am orange.
I am king of the animals.
What am I?

Answer: A lion.

Oscar Britten-Evans (5)
Emmer Green Primary School, Reading

What Am I?

I can breathe fire.
I live in a cave.
I only come out at night.
I only eat meat.
I am big.
I am scary.
What am I?

Answer: A dragon.

William Rees Musker (6)
Emmer Green Primary School, Reading

Animal

I have spots.
I have long legs.
I live in Africa.
I live by myself.
I am yellow.
I have a long tail.
What am I?

Answer: A cheetah.

William Newbury (6)
Emmer Green Primary School, Reading

What Am I?

I have a smile.
I have a swirl.
I have a nose.
I have a spot.
I have an eye.
I have a scarf.
What am I?

Answer: A gingerbread man.

Lily Rose Fearn (6)
Emmer Green Primary School, Reading

What Am I?

I have a crown.
I wear a dress.
My hair is long.
I have a pet.
I have a bad mum.
I live in a castle.
Who am I?

Answer: Rapunzel

Florence Thomas (6)
Emmer Green Primary School, Reading

Yellow

I have thunder shocks.
I have a tail whip.
I have claws.
I fight baddies.
I am yellow.
Who am I?

Answer: Pikachu.

Seth Heslop (5)
Emmer Green Primary School, Reading

What Am I?

I have wings.
I can fly.
I breathe fire.
I have spikes.
I am evil.
I am scary.
What am I?

Answer: A dragon.

Morgan Michael Fenner (5)
Emmer Green Primary School, Reading

What Am I?

I have wings.
I can do magic.
I have a hat.
I have pointy shoes.
I have long hair.
What am I?

Answer: A fairy.

Lizzie Veal (5)
Emmer Green Primary School, Reading

What Am I?

I have a sword.
I broke the spell.
I kissed Sleeping Beauty.
I found the castle.
Who am I?

Answer: A prince.

Arjun Balaji (5)
Emmer Green Primary School, Reading

Who Am I?

I can run very fast.
I was baked.
Nobody can catch me.
I am tasty.
Who am I?

Answer: The gingerbread man.

Charlie Potter (5)
Emmer Green Primary School, Reading

Who Am I?

I married a beast.
I am a princess.
I go in the woods.
I wear a dress.
Who am I?

Answer: Belle.

Iona Freya Casagranda (6)
Emmer Green Primary School, Reading

What Am I?

I breathe fire.
I can fly.
I have little horns.
I have scales.
What am I?

Answer: A dragon.

Alexandria Prior (5)
Emmer Green Primary School, Reading

What Am I?

I have wings.
I breathe fire.
I have scales.
What am I?

Answer: A dragon.

Tommy Briggs (6) & Jack Perona
Emmer Green Primary School, Reading

What Am I?

I breathe.
I breathe fire.
I have a tail.
What am I?

Answer: A dragon.

Jude McEwan (6)
Emmer Green Primary School, Reading

What Am I?

I breathe fire.
I have scales.
I can fly.
What am I?

Answer: A dragon.

Ethan Lunnon (6)
Emmer Green Primary School, Reading

What Am I?

I have wings.
I have horns.
I have fire.
what am I?

Answer: A dragon.

Joseph Unsworth (5)
Emmer Green Primary School, Reading

What Am I?

I have wings.
I have a wand.
I can fly.
What am I?

Answer: A fairy.

Megan Tayler (6), Lila Grace & Edie Marie Chard Wicks
Emmer Green Primary School, Reading

Rare Breed

Colour is my first name,
Because I'm not quite the same.
My body is full of stripes.
I also have a very scary bite.
Siberia is my natural home,
But being me, I always roam.
I have big teeth and big, sharp claws,
Sticking out of giant paws.
I know my way around the snow,
That's how I know where to go.
What am I?

Answer: A Siberian tiger.

Jessie Cuddihy Oakes (5)
Fir Tree Primary School & Nursery, Newbury

Flying High

I start in an egg, all safe in my nest.
My mummy and daddy bring me worms to eat.
A juicy worm just can't be beaten.
When I am old enough and I'm set free,
I then jump out of my safe tree.
I meet new friends,
And fly high in the sky.
If I see a human, I get a bit shy.
What am I?

Answer: A bird.

Bethany Dobson (6)
Fir Tree Primary School & Nursery, Newbury

Cheeky

I live on the land,
And swing from a tree.
I run around and like to be free.
There is lots of drama,
If I don't get my banana.
I live with my mumma,
And my pappa.
Sometimes I go ooo, ooh, aah, aah!
What am I?

Answer: A monkey.

Aimee May (6)
Fir Tree Primary School & Nursery, Newbury

Swinging Into The Jungle

I can swing on trees.
I eat plants and insects.
I live in tropical forests.
I have strong arms, a massive chest,
And broad hands and feet.
I am covered in long, thick, black hair,
And I am strong.
What am I?

Answer: A gorilla.

Deshane Elliott
Fir Tree Primary School & Nursery, Newbury

Roarsome

I have whiskers and I roar.
You can find me outdoors.
I live on grassy plains
With a few trees for a change.
My fur is sandy and light.
The end of my tail is as dark as night.
What am I?

Answer: A lion.

Isla Barville (5)
Fir Tree Primary School & Nursery, Newbury

What Am I?

I am blubbery and wet.
I am grey and wild.
I like to splash.
Pinocchio was in my belly.
My dear old mum, they called her Nelly.
You may find I rhyme with tail.
What am I?

Answer: A whale.

Ruby-Lee Amelia Evans (6)

Fir Tree Primary School & Nursery, Newbury

Hunt

I live in the woods,
And I hunt at night.
Chasing all the chickens in sight.
I have pointy ears,
A pointy nose,
And a long, bushy tail.
My fur is orange.
What am I?

Answer: A fox.

Lola Holmes (6)
Fir Tree Primary School & Nursery, Newbury

What Am I?

I can fly but I don't have feathers.
I have spots but I'm not sick.
I have sticky feet.
I am a type of beetle.
I am a lady, but also a 'he'.
What am I?

Answer: A ladybird.

Ace Sprules (5)
Fir Tree Primary School & Nursery, Newbury

Mushy

I grow in gardens.
I am nice to eat.
I am sweet.
A flower shares my name.
My colour is green.
I am small and round.
I am nice with fish and chips.
What am I?

Answer: A pea.

Gregory Peter Rosewarne (6)

Fir Tree Primary School & Nursery, Newbury

Live In The Wild

I live in Africa.
I'm also seen in zoos in England.
I am a tall animal.
I have spots.
I have the longest neck of any animal.
What am I?

Answer: A giraffe.

Ashton Alexander (5)

Fir Tree Primary School & Nursery, Newbury

Who Am I?

I have two legs.
I have two sharp hands.
My body is green.
I run fast.
My eyes are green.
I live in the forest.
What am I?

Answer: A dinosaur.

Mariyam Fatima Ahmed (6)
Fir Tree Primary School & Nursery, Newbury

Big And Hungry

I have very sharp teeth.
I eat other animals.
I have a very long tail.
I lived 65 million years ago.
I eat meat.
What am I?

Answer: A T-rex.

Daniel Freeman (5)

Fir Tree Primary School & Nursery, Newbury

Wonder Pet

I am a pet.
I have four legs.
I like to run.
I like to bark.
I have a tail,
And I like to wiggle it.
What am I?

Answer: A dog.

Noor Mohamed (6)
Fir Tree Primary School & Nursery, Newbury

What's The Time?

I have a big, wet nose.
I have a fluffy tail.
I am grey.
I eat meat.
I live in the forest.
What am I?

Answer: A wolf.

Millie Richens (6)
Fir Tree Primary School & Nursery, Newbury

What Am I?

I have a thumb,
And four fingers,
But I am not alive.
What am I?

Answer: A glove.

Riley John Cotter (6)
Fir Tree Primary School & Nursery, Newbury

Boom, Bang And Crackle

People say oooo,
People say aahh,
When they see me.
I'm usually quite far.
Sometimes I'm quiet,
But usually, I'm loud!
When I am out,
There's always a crowd.
I'm lovely to look at,
But you must stay back!
I will amaze you when the sky is black!
I only appear on special nights.
You won't miss me because I am so bright!
What am I?

Answer: A firework.

Harrison Durkan (7)
Our Lady Of Peace Catholic Infant & Nursery
School, Slough

What Am I?

I am small and definitely round.
I show you the way you want to go.
I am not a clock but really close.
I have one arrow on me.
I am not a big, tall building that has a clock,
But the clue is I am nearly a clock.
When you stand up you're going to see that.
The arrow moves faster and faster around,
And when it stops,
You will see where you go.
What am I?

Answer: A compass.

Apolonia Łucja Marszałek (6)
Our Lady Of Peace Catholic Infant & Nursery
School, Slough

Good Climb

I am a type of big cat.
I am a large, strong mammal.
I run up to 35mph.
I can't climb as good as a leopard.
I can lift a log.
I love the snow and water.
I eat deer, sloths, bears, lions, dogs and snakes.
I live in China, that is in Asia.
If I am a female, I end with 'ess'.
What am I?

Answer: A South China tiger.

Jigar Saini (6)
Our Lady Of Peace Catholic Infant & Nursery School, Slough

Heat Power!

I make the flowers grow, grow, grow,
But not any cold, white snow.
Most people eat ice cream,
While the sun shines and beams.
The splendid sun shining in the sky,
And the children play nearby.
I have longer days and shorter nights,
And sometimes little bugs bite.

Answer: Summer.

David Narh-Dorh (7)

Our Lady Of Peace Catholic Infant & Nursery
School, Slough

Fast Runner

I have black stripes.
I live in the jungle.
I also have white stripes.
I am a mammal.
I'm hot-blooded.
I might look like a horse.
I live near trees that are green.
I might make a sound like a horse.
I have eyes that are white and black.
What am I?

Answer: A zebra.

Musa Asif (7)
Our Lady Of Peace Catholic Infant & Nursery School, Slough

Feathery Beauty

I have a wingspan of five metres.
I'm from the Phasianidae family.
You will find me in India, Africa,
And Southeast Asia.
My namesake is the same as a female,
Of this exotic species in Hindi.
I have eye-catching, exquisite feathers.
What am I?

Answer: A peahen.

Mayuri Nathini Das (7)
Our Lady Of Peace Catholic Infant & Nursery
School, Slough

An Object

I have a light but I am not a torch.
I have cars but I am not a car truck.
I have bumps but I am not a wiggly canal.
I have roads but I am not a car park.
I have stands but I'm not a bed.
I have sharp teeth but I am not a monster.
What am I?

Answer: A racing track.

Hadi Asif (7)

Our Lady Of Peace Catholic Infant & Nursery
School, Slough

I Will Keep You Warm

I like snow.
Do you find me on my own?
No! No! Never alone.
With my friends, we fill the place,
From one end to another end.
When we see wavy grass, we run fast.
There's nothing left after us.
Out of my hair, jumpers are made.
What am I?

Answer: A sheep.

Coco Janot (7)
Our Lady Of Peace Catholic Infant & Nursery
School, Slough

Savannah Scandal

I don't eat meat.
I don't have two legs.
I have four legs.
I eat leaves.
I have black spots on me.
I have tiny ears.
I have tiny legs.
I have a long neck.
I am a mammal.
I have fur.
I have yellow skin.
What am I?

Answer: A giraffe.

Sanjana Podigala (7)
Our Lady Of Peace Catholic Infant & Nursery
School, Slough

A Yummy Sweet

It can come in any shape and size.
You can eat it or mix it in a drink.
It can be named after space.
A gift to give and share.
A Santa, an egg or a reindeer.
Everyone loves it so much.
Children and grown-ups.
What is it?

Answer: Chocolate.

Aapti Vij (5)
Our Lady Of Peace Catholic Infant & Nursery
School, Slough

Who Am I?

Based on 'My Mother' by Ann Taylor

Who sat and watched my infant head,
When sleeping on my crocodile bed?
When pain and sickness made me cry,
Who gazed upon my heavy eye?
Who taught my infant lips to pray,
And love God's holy book?
Who am I?

Answer: My mother.

Kamsi C Isi (7)
Our Lady Of Peace Catholic Infant & Nursery
School, Slough

On The Farm

I am famous on the farm,
With lots of spots on the front and back.
I am white and black, sometimes brown.
I love to eat grass on the field.
If you need a drink, come to me.
I have lots of creamy milk.
What am I?

Answer: A cow.

Zuzanna Pajdzik (7)
Our Lady Of Peace Catholic Infant & Nursery
School, Slough

Fast Object

I go really fast.
I have four black, big wheels.
I drive on a huge race track,
And if I need fuel
I go to the pit stop.
I have lots of fans,
And only professional drivers can drive me.
What am I?

Answer: A racing car.

Anish Mandal (6)

Our Lady Of Peace Catholic Infant & Nursery
School, Slough

A Furry Cub

I live in a cave.
I am a scary animal.
I eat fish.
I am a carnivorous animal.
I walk flat-footed like humans.
I give birth to my cubs.
I go into a long hibernation.
What am I?

Answer: A bear.

Makayla Korkor Bah-Nartey (7)
Our Lady Of Peace Catholic Infant & Nursery
School, Slough

Soak Me

I have holes in my top and bottom.
My left and right and my middle,
But I still hold water.
I can be yellow.
I can dry things.
I can be made into a bath toy.
What am I?

Answer: A sponge.

Simon Maradze (7)
Our Lady Of Peace Catholic Infant & Nursery
School, Slough

Transformers

I can transform.
I am on the Cartoon Network.
I can turn into a jet.
I am purple and dark blue.
I am a Decepticon.
I am on the TV show, Transformers.
Who am I?

Answer: Soundwave.

Ugochukwu Uchenna Eze (7)
Our Lady Of Peace Catholic Infant & Nursery
School, Slough

Too Long Legs

I am furry and dry.
I can hang around upside down.
I sleep at daytime,
And play at night.
I have two long legs,
And two short legs.
What am I?

Answer: A two-toed sloth.

Miguel Christopher Quebral (5)

Our Lady Of Peace Catholic Infant & Nursery
School, Slough

Read My Words

You can turn my pages.
Flip me over for ages.
Read my words.
Jump for joy.
Just before you turn off the light,
You can read me a story.
What am I?

Answer: A book.

Amelia Page (6)

Our Lady Of Peace Catholic Infant & Nursery
School, Slough

The Crime

I see you.
I have very good sight.
I am blue and bright green.
I go on a fast motorbike,
And in a car.
I am loud.
Who am I?

Answer: A policeman.

Isabelle Ahanon (5)

Our Lady Of Peace Catholic Infant & Nursery
School, Slough

What Am I?

I have a very long neck.
I'm from Africa.
I have brown spots.
I am tall.
I am a herbivore.
I am also a mammal.
What am I?

Answer: A giraffe.

Lauren Fualefac (6)
Our Lady Of Peace Catholic Infant & Nursery
School, Slough

Cat

I have big teeth.
I have black stripes.
I eat meat.
I have sharp claws.
I live in India.
I have a loud roar.
What am I?

Answer: A tiger.

Tianna-Rose Kalirai (6)
Our Lady Of Peace Catholic Infant & Nursery
School, Slough

What Am I?

I live in a jungle.
I am fierce.
I bite.
I snap.
I grrrr.
I am scary.
I sleep in a river.
What am I?

Answer: A crocodile.

Annabel Lomas (7)
Our Lady Of Peace Catholic Infant & Nursery
School, Slough

Pride

I am good at running.
I have fur.
I have a dotted colour.
I live in a forest,
And I have four legs.
What am I?

Answer: A cheetah.

Timizo Nganga (7)
Our Lady Of Peace Catholic Infant & Nursery School, Slough

The Tall One

I have a long neck.
I live in Africa.
I have a long tongue.
I eat trees.
I have four legs.
What am I?

Answer: A giraffe.

Roxi Hasley (5)

Our Lady Of Peace Catholic Infant & Nursery
School, Slough

Squeezy Thing

My mummy said I can't have it,
And I never have it with eggs.
It is red.
It is squeezy.
What is it?

Answer: Ketchup.

Bruno Valek (7)

Our Lady Of Peace Catholic Infant & Nursery
School, Slough

Sky Fluffy

I can fly but have no wings.
I can cry but I have no eyes.
Where I go,
Darkness follows me.
What am I?

Answer: A cloud.

Muhammad Ashraf (6)
Our Lady Of Peace Catholic Infant & Nursery
School, Slough

New

I'm small and cute.
I crawl on the floor.
I cry a lot.
I sleep in the day and night.
What am I?

Answer: A baby.

Gabriel Wojchiech Dubiel (7)
Our Lady Of Peace Catholic Infant & Nursery
School, Slough

What Am I?

I can open like a door.
I'm black and white,
And read a lot.
What am I?

Answer: A book.

Sirien Jabr (7)

Our Lady Of Peace Catholic Infant & Nursery
School, Slough

Tricky Animal Riddle

I begin with a B.
I can fly up in the sky.
I have four colours on my wings.
I love to take nectar from the flower.
My predator is a bird.
I end with a Y.
I can lunge from side to side.
I am an animal which flies.
I have colours on my wings.
My middle letter is an E.
I have two big wings and two small wings.
What am I?

Answer: A butterfly.

Humna Kashif Siddiquei (7)
Parlaunt Park Primary School, Slough

The Winter Snow Riddle

I am fluffy,
And I camouflage very well in the snow.
I start with S but end with a B.
I am a herbivore.
It's very hard to find food in the snow.
I give birth once in a year.
We snuggle together to keep warm.
I live in the Arctic.
I am white.
There are many of me.
I have a thick coat.
What am I?

Answer: A bunny.

Simranjit Saggu (6)
Parlaunt Park Primary School, Slough

Jungle Animal

I roar when I am angry.
I close my mouth to attack.
I eat meat for food.
I have many curves.
I am fast when I run.
I have black stripes.
I am very strong.
I have a curved tail.
I have soft fur.
My claws are sharp.
I can balance on a paw.
I lick water to drink.
What am I?

Answer: A tiger.

Sahil Bhatia (6)
Parlaunt Park Primary School, Slough

What Am I?

I fly in the blue sky.
I am a very big scavenger.
I might be endangered.
I fly like a giant bird.
I have a giant beak.
I have two giant wings,
And I also have two long feet.
I have a belly.
I have two small eyes.
I have two little bones,
And I am a massive bird.
What am I?

Answer: A vulture.

Klaudia Jonderko (6)
Parlaunt Park Primary School, Slough

Who Am I?

I live with my family in a brown herd.
I have a black and white stripy coat,
But I don't sleep in a boat.
I have long pointy ears,
But I don't have tears.
I'm not a carnivore,
But I'm a herbivore.
I have black eyes like the night.
I live next to the lions.
What am I?

Answer: A zebra.

Sreya Aji (7)
Parlaunt Park Primary School, Slough

Guess My Animal

My name begins with an F,
But I am from the Arctic.
I am from the cat family.
I curl up into a circle when I sleep.
I eat very small animals,
Like lemmings and other bugs.
I am a scavenger,
And I sometimes look for food.
I eat leftover organs from animals.
What am I?

Answer: An Arctic fox.

Shanzay Aslam (6)
Parlaunt Park Primary School, Slough

What Am I?

I am a meat eater.
I eat red meat.
I hunt in the dark night,
And I fight.
I am a patterned carnivore.
I have green and soft skin.
I am happy to hunt.
I live in an immense, colossal jungle.
I like to drink cold, soaking water.
I don't talk.
What am I?

Answer: A viper snake.

Muhammad Salaar Moosa (6)
Parlaunt Park Primary School, Slough

Tricky Trocky Riddle

I begin with a B,
And end with a Y.
I go to flowers and take pollen from them.
I have four beautiful wings.
My natural habitat is a rainforest,
But I'm also found here.
I have beautiful patterns on my wings.
I am sometimes different sizes.
What am I?

Answer: A butterfly.

Shaivi Prasad (7)
Parlaunt Park Primary School, Slough

Slithery Things

I am very long.
I can shed all my skin.
I smell with my tongue.
I have thin, smooth, beautiful skin.
I lay small, white, tiny eggs.
There's no possible chance I can have legs.
I might squeeze my prey.
I can't walk.
I can't crawl.
What am I?

Answer: A snake.

Padmakali Chaudhuri (6)
Parlaunt Park Primary School, Slough

Stinging Sniper

I have a yellow barb.
I use a pincer.
I have big snippers.
I glow under sunlight.
I eat insects.
I have twelve eyes.
I am 19cm.
I have eight legs.
I eat termites.
I can give a nasty nip.
I can be a pet.
I am skinny.
What am I?

Answer: A scorpion.

Rayan El-Taki (7)
Parlaunt Park Primary School, Slough

Guess My Answer

My name starts with a T.
I am famous.
I live underground.
I hunt at night.
I do not spin webs.
I have hair.
There are 900 species of me.
I am found in parts of America and Africa.
I eat insects, beetles and grasshoppers.
What am I?

Answer: A tarantula.

Navin Singh Dhinsay (6)
Parlaunt Park Primary School, Slough

The Killer Of The Water

I come from the jungle.
I have a fierce snap.
I have sharp, bladed teeth.
I am scary, so be nimble and run.
I hunt for my prey.
My jaw is hard so I am tough.
My brain is sharp, so watch out.
I look like a rock and water.
What am I?

Answer: A crocodile.

Samardeep Singh Bhagtana (6)
Parlaunt Park Primary School, Slough

Tropical Animal Riddle

I have four colourful wings.
I range in size from an eighth of an inch,
To twelve inches.
My wings are full of patterns.
I fly around and drink pollen.
I can be little and very big.
I begin with a B.
What am I?

Answer: A butterfly.

Zara Szarvas-Jones (7)
Parlaunt Park Primary School, Slough

What Am I?

I live in the Arctic.
I snatch other animals' food.
I have a thick, warm coat.
I have a thick, warm tail.
I eat small animals.
I weigh between 3 and 8kg.
I can hear from over one mile away.
What am I?

Answer: An Arctic fox.

Sophie Brennan (6)
Parlaunt Park Primary School, Slough

What Do You Think I Am?

I am strong, huge and wild.
You can find me in a rainforest,
With black and orange stripes.
I have fluffy fur.
I have a short tail,
And I am very fast.
I have paws,
And I have sharp teeth.
What am I?

Answer: A tiger.

Rehan Siddique Shahzad (7)
Parlaunt Park Primary School, Slough

Daisy's Powerful Riddle!

I look like a seal but bigger.
I live by the Arctic Circle.
I live by the sea in the cold ice.
I have two tusks that help me climb over the ice.
I am a mammal.
I have animal friends by the ice.
What am I?

Answer: A walrus.

Daisy Kirby (7)
Parlaunt Park Primary School, Slough

Guess My Animal

I am hairy and spiky.
I am creepy and poisonous.
I crawl when I walk.
I can climb on walls.
I can't change colour.
I sting and I am endangered.
I live by myself.
I am grey.
What am I?

Answer: A tarantula.

Walid Alqaysi (7)
Parlaunt Park Primary School, Slough

What Am I?

I am very hairy.
I live in a big or small burrow.
I do not spin webs.
I have big legs to move around.
I am not that big.
I start with a T.
I am a kind of spider.
What am I?

Answer: A tarantula.

Gabriel Justin Toma (7)
Parlaunt Park Primary School, Slough

The Hard Riddle

I don't harm insects and humans.
I bring peace and harmony.
I am as big as a coin and a leaf.
I eat pollen.
I begin with a B.
I have four wings.
What am I?

Answer: A butterfly.

Riley Tearle-Reardon (7)
Parlaunt Park Primary School, Slough

Big, Hairy Spider

My name starts with a T.
I have eight legs.
I live in a burrow.
I eat insects, grasshoppers and beetles.
I am very hairy.
I am a night-time hunter.
What am I?

Answer: A tarantula.

Gurdeep Singh Virdee (6)
Parlaunt Park Primary School, Slough

What Am I?

I have white and black stripes.
I have a spiky mane.
I have a positive herd.
I live on the African plains.
I live in a hot place.
I have a family.
What am I?

Answer: A zebra.

Safa Ghauri (7)
Parlaunt Park Primary School, Slough

Who Am I?

My name starts with the letter S.
I live in the snow.
I have a little beak.
I live in the Antarctic.
I can fly and I have two wings.
What am I?

Answer: A snowy owl.

Solha Stoor (6)
Parlaunt Park Primary School, Slough

Tricky Animal Riddle

I live underground.

I spin silk, not webs.

My venom is milder than a honeybee.

I eat beetles and grasshoppers.

I am 9 and 28g.

What am I?

Answer: A tarantula.

Ritwik Mukherjee (6)

Parlaunt Park Primary School, Slough

Great Flyer

I eat fish.
I live in the Arctic.
I am from the bird family.
I can turn my head.
I have big eyes.
I have sharp claws.
What am I?

Answer: A snowy owl.

Amelia Eileen Warren-Searle (6)
Parlaunt Park Primary School, Slough

Guess My Answer

I have a purple tongue.
I have brown splodges on me.
I also have yellow skin.
I have orange eyes.
I have a large neck.
What am I?

Answer: A giraffe.

Keira Grace Chopra (7)
Parlaunt Park Primary School, Slough

Bird

I eat fish.
I can turn around.
I am a bird of prey.
I have big eyes, a good grip,
And I am a great flyer.
What am I?

Answer: A snowy owl.

Noor Awan (7)
Parlaunt Park Primary School, Slough

Green Animal

My name starts with an L.
I am green.
I am a reptile.
I have a long tongue.
I eat flies.
I am small.
What am I?

Answer: A lizard.

Billy Edmonds (7)
Parlaunt Park Primary School, Slough

The Colourful, Beautiful, Best Animals

I have four wings.
I fly from flower to flower.
I'm very colourful.
I like flying.
What am I?

Answer: A butterfly.

Umayma Hedayet (6)
Parlaunt Park Primary School, Slough

What Am I?

My name starts with a B.
I live in the rainforest,
And I like to fly.
What am I?

Answer: A butterfly.

Briony Mcintyre (7)
Parlaunt Park Primary School, Slough

I Scare The Fish

I have short arms and long legs.
My teeth are as big as pegs.
My tail is longer than my legs.
I have a spine along my back,
I break things with a whack.
I am scary when I roar,
It makes other dinosaurs fall to the floor.
The world was different when I was alive,
Humans hadn't learned to thrive.
I like to eat fish,
But not from a dish.
What am I?

Answer: A spinosaurus.

Benjy Everett (7)
St Michael's CE Primary School, Sunninghill

Fluffy Power

I am fluffy, puffy and imaginative.
People think I'm funny,
But I am as sweet as honey.
I have a long, white mane,
And I really don't like the rain.
My favourite colour is pink,
And when you see me I will give you a wink.
I have a long, white horn,
That sparkles at the sight of dawn.

Answer: A unicorn.

India Star McNair (6)
St Michael's CE Primary School, Sunninghill

Out Of This World

I am a creature with a green face.
I visit this world from outer space.
I have big antennas and crazy eyes.
I land my spaceship down from the skies.
It's a flying visit, might see you soon.
I have to get back for my dinner on the moon.
What am I?

Answer: An alien.

Phoebe Powell (7)
St Michael's CE Primary School, Sunninghill

Slow Mixed

When darkness comes, I wake,
Ready to catch my food.
I swoop down and grab my mouse.
I go back to my tree hole,
Swallowing it in one gulp.
Going back to sleep as the sun rises.
I have feathers
And I can fly.
What am I?

Answer: An owl.

Anya Carroll (7)
St Michael's CE Primary School, Sunninghill

My Magical Friend

I can fly through the sky.
I look beautiful all the time.
You will find me in a forest.
I make some fairy and butterfly friends.
When I fly, I create a rainbow.
I have amazing wings,
And a magic horn.
What am I?

Answer: A unicorn.

Daisy Dyer (7)
St Michael's CE Primary School, Sunninghill

Fruity Tutti

I am yummy.
Connie puts me in her tummy.
I am served cold.
Drink me before I get too cold.
I am not rough.
Connie can't get enough.
I am made with squashed fruit,
But not with a boot!
What am I?

Answer: A smoothie.

Connie Neal (7)
St Michael's CE Primary School, Sunninghill

A Fluffy Friend

I live outdoors in a field.
I have a furry and fluffy coat,
That keeps me warm.
I'm most active at dusk.
I really like to eat grass.
I get around by hopping.
I have a twitchy nose.
What am I?

Answer: A bunny.

Isabella Rose Sousa (6)
St Michael's CE Primary School, Sunninghill

Untitled

Birds build nests in me.
Bits of me can fall off,
And change colour.
I have a trunk.
You bring me in your house at Christmas.
I have bark.
I am full of sap.
What am I?

Answer: A tree.

Alexander Cunnison (6)
St Michael's CE Primary School, Sunninghill

YoungWriters

Red All Over

I grow in the garden.
I am ripe and juicy.
I have green on my head.
I have about 200 seeds on me.
I am a member of the rose family.
I grow on a vine.
What am I?

Answer: A strawberry.

Molly Isabella Stokes (7)
St Michael's CE Primary School, Sunninghill

Suitable For All

I play well with everybody.
You can take me apart.
One day, I'm a car.
The next, I'm a house.
I can be as big as a mountain,
Or as small as a mouse.
What am I?

Answer: Lego.

Theo Rose (7)
St Michael's CE Primary School, Sunninghill

What Am I?

I am extremely dangerous.
I can gulp you up in one second.
I have an enormous body.
My mouth is a gigantic mouth.
You would be much smaller than me.
What am I?

Answer: An anaconda.

Nancy Neal (5)
St Michael's CE Primary School, Sunninghill

Magic

I have a wand.
I fly very high.
I have a pink bunny with wings.
I am the queen of the sky.
I have sparkly fairy dust.
I have a friend, a mermaid.
What am I?

Answer: A fairy.

Megan Lloyd (7)
St Michael's CE Primary School, Sunninghill

Part Of The Family!

He is cuddly.
He is white and orange.
He is one year old.
He has a girlfriend.
He lives in my house.
He likes going in his hammock.
Who is he?

Answer: My pet cat.

Anish Nehra (7)
St Michael's CE Primary School, Sunninghill

What Am I?

I have four long legs.
I have big, brown spots.
I have short ears,
And little hooves.
I have got four of them.
What am I?

Answer: A giraffe.

Jessica Smith (5)

St Michael's CE Primary School, Sunninghill

What Am I?

I have patterns on my back.
My skin is smooth.
I live in the jungle.
I have no legs.
I am thin.
What am I?

Answer: A snake.

Zara McSharry (6)
St Michael's CE Primary School, Sunninghill

What Am I?

I have cute eyes.
I ride on my mummy's back.
I sometimes get lost.
I climb trees.
What am I?

Answer: A monkey.

Hannah Michelle Williams (5)
St Michael's CE Primary School, Sunninghill

What Am I?

I have four long legs.
I have spots on me.
I am yellow.
I have a long neck.
What am I?

Answer: A giraffe.

Poppy Dyer (6)
St Michael's CE Primary School, Sunninghill

What Am I?

I have four legs.
I have a brown tummy.
I am very cheeky.
I love bananas.
What am I?

Answer: A monkey.

Ethan Smyth (6)
St Michael's CE Primary School, Sunninghill

What Am I?

I have short legs.
I am big.
I am a little bit spiky.
I have a fluffy tail.
What am I?

Answer: A lion.

Charlie Kemp (6)
St Michael's CE Primary School, Sunninghill

What Am I?

I am black.
I have eight legs.
I can shoot webs.
I have a round body.
What am I?

Answer: A spider.

Theo Simmonds (5)
St Michael's CE Primary School, Sunninghill

What Am I?

I can eat people.
I can be any colour.
I sometimes hide on top of the tree.
What am I?

Answer: A snake.

Louis Fowler (5)
St Michael's CE Primary School, Sunninghill

What Am I?

I have four legs.
I run fast.
I live in Africa.
I have spots.
What am I?

Answer: A cheetah.

Elizabeth Rowat (6)
St Michael's CE Primary School, Sunninghill

What Am I?

I am very strong.
I am black.
I have two ears.
I am heavy.
What am I?

Answer: A gorilla.

Eliza Read (6)
St Michael's CE Primary School, Sunninghill

Snowman

I am a very cold man.
I am made out of snow.
Snowflakes fall on me.
I have a carrot nose.
I have three black spots on my body.
I melt in the snow.
I have three pieces on my body.
What am I?

Answer: A snowman.

Caleb Erasmus (6)
The King's House School, Windsor

What Am I?

I have seeds,
And if you eat me, I can be sweet.
I am a colour and a fruit.
I can roll like a ball.
I can be peeled or cut into pieces.
I am served at breakfast as a juice.
What am I?

Answer: An orange.

Grace Ravelo (7)
The King's House School, Windsor

What Am I?

I have things that go round and round,
And things that make a sound.
I have five wheels,
And one makes me turn to get to places.
I have super speed when there is a need.
What am I?

Answer: A police car.

Jesse Daniel Rademeyer (6)
The King's House School, Windsor

The King Of The World

He is a creator,
Just not like a painter.
He soars in the sky,
And helps people as he passes by.
He is in charge of something large,
And is part of the Trinity.
Who is he?

Answer: God.

Evelyn Shaya (6)
The King's House School, Windsor

Dry Defence

I keep you dry.
I am small or big.
I am waterproof.
I can be any colour.
I can be a wheel shape or tube.
I have a button to push me up.
What am I?

Answer: An umbrella.

Daniel Richards (6)

The King's House School, Windsor

What Am I?

I have a long neck.
I eat trees.
I walk all over the savannah.
I have the best view in the world.
I have long eyelashes.
I am yellow.
What am I?

Answer: A giraffe.

Jessica Costa (6)
The King's House School, Windsor

Animal Or Car?

I am part of the cat family.
I like sitting in trees.
I am camouflaged.
I have a cub.
I live in the Americas.
I eat meat.
What am I?

Answer: A jaguar.

Hugo Holmes-Clough (5)
The King's House School, Windsor

Ninja

I am green and I swim.
I eat leaves from the sea.
I eat fish.
I have armour.
I live by the ocean.
I walk slowly.
What am I?

Answer: A turtle.

Harriet Holmes-Clough (7)
The King's House School, Windsor

Fiery And Hot!

I have burning, red eyes.
I can spit fire out.
I can fly.
I have wings.
I have spikes on my back.
I am green.
What am I?

Answer: A dragon.

Patricio Taylor (7)
The King's House School, Windsor

Who Am I?

I have scales.
My fiery breath burns.
I'm angry and red.
I'm scary and big.
I live in a cave.
What am I?

Answer: A dragon.

Elizabeth Harding (6)
The King's House School, Windsor

Big And Scary

I am hairy.
I am scary.
I eat honey.
I have big claws.
I live in a cave.
What am I?

Answer: A bear.

Alex Welch-Torino (6)
The King's House School, Windsor

Mystery Creature

I have a horn that has different colours,
Like blue, pink and purple.
I have white skin.
I have multicoloured hair.
I have quite a lot of children.
I live in the wild.
I hunt for my food.
What am I?

Answer: A unicorn.

Stephanie Ann Simon (7)
Waverley School, Finchampstead

On The Road

I have four wheels and tyres.
I have a driver's seat.
I have seventeen passenger seats.
I have two doors.
I have a windscreen.
I have six lights.
I have ten windows.
What am I?

Answer: A school bus.

Edward Hinitt (6)
Waverley School, Finchampstead

Swimming Ocean

I sing in the ocean.
I breathe underwater.
I love going on adventures with my pet fish.
My tail's colour is lime green.
My fish's colour is yellow with blue stripes.
What am I?

Answer: A mermaid.

Eva Hope (6)
Waverley School, Finchampstead

Diving

I can dive a lot.
I live in the open ocean.
I am normally grey.
I have fins.
I like the water.
I like to dive in front of boats.
My favourite food is fish.
What am I?

Answer: A dolphin.

Eleanor Woolger (6)
Waverley School, Finchampstead

Sky Power

I am a yellow, twinkly thing.
I look very small.
I am out at night-time.
I sleep in the day.
I am there when children are asleep.
I am awake at night-time.
What am I?

Answer: A star.

Leo Lightstone (5)
Waverley School, Finchampstead

Air Craft

I can go to Australia in 48 minutes.
I have ten engines.
I am fast.
I am made in the future.
I can carry 359 people.
I go up and then down.
What am I?

Answer: A ten-engine plane.

Antar Pabla (6)
Waverley School, Finchampstead

Pool Day

I can swim in the sea.
I can sing beautifully.
I can dance in the sea.
I can't go on land.
I have a sequin tail.
My tummy button sticks out.
What am I?

Answer: A mermaid.

Imogen Nicol (6)
Waverley School, Finchampstead

Swimming Power

You can see me swim.
You can see me in a tank.
I live in the ocean.
I might be a pet.
I like eating fishy food.
I am covered in scales.
What am I?

Answer: A goldfish.

Niki Pittock (6)
Waverley School, Finchampstead

Flap Your Wings

I suck pollen.
I am small.
I come in all colours.
I fly as high as a roof.
I started off as a caterpillar.
I live in hot countries.
What am I?

Answer: A butterfly.

Sofia Beet (7)
Waverley School, Finchampstead

Forest Field

You can see me if you are silent.
If you are noisy, I run away.
I have four legs.
I eat grass.
I have antlers.
My baby is called a fawn.
What am I?

Answer: A deer.

Catherine Agar (5)
Waverley School, Finchampstead

Stomp Down The Castle

I am very big.
I eat you!
I have sharp claws.
I have sharp teeth.
I lived a very long time ago.
I was the king of the dinosaurs.
What am I?

Answer: A T-rex.

Esmé Walsh (6)
Waverley School, Finchampstead

Stomping Power

I am very big.
I have a trunk.
My favourite food is plants.
I used to live in the jungle.
I have tusks.
I am furry.
What am I?

Answer: A woolly mammoth.

Vasu Gupta (6)
Waverley School, Finchampstead

Writing Power

You can write with me.
You can sharpen me.
I have a sharp end.
I can come in all sorts of colours.
You can do homework with me.
What am I?

Answer: A pencil.

Sophia Fadden (6)
Waverley School, Finchampstead

The Sea

I live in the sea.
I spurt water.
I eat fish and krill.
I am an ocean giant.
I swim in cold waters.
I navigate with sound.
What am I?

Answer: A whale.

Alessa (6)
Waverley School, Finchampstead

Swimming

I like to swim.
I have gills.
I live in seaweed.
I have fins.
My friend is a mermaid.
I can be lots of different colours.
What am I?

Answer: A fish.

Hannah Rowsell (6)
Waverley School, Finchampstead

A Farm Friend

I am a friend.
You can ride on me.
You can stroke me.
You can find me on a farm.
You can feed me.
I have a tail.
What am I?

Answer: A horse.

Jo Tan (5)
Waverley School, Finchampstead

Whoosh

You can sit in me.
I am made out of metal.
I have a point at the end of me.
I can fly very fast.
I go into space.
What am I?

Answer: A spaceship.

Imogen Avery (5)
Waverley School, Finchampstead

Soil Creatures

I am red.
I eat lots of things.
I am very tiny.
I bundle in a big group.
I bite people.
I have six legs.
What am I?

Answer: A red ant.

Tommy German (5)
Waverley School, Finchampstead

In The Future

I can hover.
I can't go on water.
You do not have me in this world.
I look like the bottom of a scooter.
What am I?

Answer: A hoverboard.

Fraser Boulton (5)
Waverley School, Finchampstead

My Best Friend

I am a girl.
I have four legs.
I have green eyes.
I am black.
I have fur.
I have pointy ears.
Who am I?

Answer: Pippa's cat.

Pippa Ellen Dickinson (5)
Waverley School, Finchampstead

Animal Power

I can roar.
I am yellowy brown.
I am strong.
I have a mane.
I have long claws.
I live in the jungle.
What am I?

Answer: A lion.

Beau Murphy (6)
Waverley School, Finchampstead

Wag Power

I have four legs.
I have long ears.
I walk on a lead.
I eat from a bowl.
I am furry.
I am a pet.
What am I?

Answer: A dog.

Emily Neale (5)
Waverley School, Finchampstead

Black And White

I am furry.
I can climb.
I live in the forest.
I have black rings around my eyes.
I eat bamboo.
What am I?

Answer: A panda.

Max Sully (5)
Waverley School, Finchampstead

Hopper

Watch me dig.
I am white.
I eat carrots.
I hop on the grass.
I can be a pet.
I am soft.
What am I?

Answer: A rabbit.

Lyra Brooks (5)
Waverley School, Finchampstead

On The Farm

I am heavy.
Children can ride on me.
I have four legs.
My legs are heavy.
My face is long.
What am I?

Answer: A horse.

Caitlin Bonnett (5)
Waverley School, Finchampstead

Flying Power

You can go on holiday in me.
I go in the air.
I have wings.
I come in lots of colours.
What am I?

Answer: An aeroplane.

Isaac Stephens (6)
Waverley School, Finchampstead

On The Sea

You can sleep on me.
You can sail on me.
I have an engine.
I can go on the sea.
What am I?

Answer: A boat.

Charlie Cox (6)
Waverley School, Finchampstead

YoungWriters
Est.1991

YOUNG WRITERS INFORMATION

We hope you have enjoyed reading this book – and that you will continue to in the coming years.

If you're a young writer who enjoys reading and creative writing, or the parent of an enthusiastic poet or story writer, do visit our website **www.youngwriters.co.uk**. Here you will find free competitions, workshops and games, as well as recommended reads, a poetry glossary and our blog.

If you would like to order further copies of this book, or any of our other titles, then please give us a call or visit **www.youngwriters.co.uk**.

Young Writers
Remus House
Coltsfoot Drive
Peterborough
PE2 9BF
(01733) 890066
info@youngwriters.co.uk